Postcards Home
A Kid's Guide To Trondheim, Norway

Photography by John D. Weigand
Poetry by Penelope Dyan

Bellissima Publishing, LLC
Jamul, California
www.bellissimapublishing.com

Copyright © 2017 by Penny D. Weigand and John D. Weigand

All rights reserved. No part of this book may be
reproduced or transmitted in any form or by any means,
electronic or mechanical, including photocopying,
recording, or by any other means, or by any information or
storage retrieval system, without permission from the publisher.

ISBN 978-1-61477-278-1
First Edition

"Nature always wears
the colors of the spirit."

Ralph Waldo Emerson

Postcards Home
Bellissima Publishing, LLC

Introduction

Trondheim, Norway is a small city on the Trondheim Fjord in central Norway. It dates back to the 11th century, and you can see the Gothic Nidaros Cathedral there. Nearby, is the Archbishop's Palace Museum with archaeological displays, as well as sculptures that include gargoyles removed from the cathedral. There are other museums and things to see here, but what is so very special about this place is everywhere you look you can snap a postcard perfect picture! And this is why this book was named "Postcards Home."

Enjoy this fun 'learn to read book' with its extra large print that is easy for young eyes to see, and see some of what award winning author, and former teacher, Penelope Dyan, and photographer, John D. Weigand, saw when they visited Trondheim, Norway, a postcard picture perfect lttle town by the sea.

Let your imagination soar like a sailboat in the wind, and have fun as you learn; because if learning isn't fun, a kid won't love to learn! Then when you are all finished with this book, watch the free music video that goes along with this book that you can find on Bellissimavideo's YouTube Channel.

Postcards Home
Bellissima Publishing, LLC

Postcards Home
A Kid's Guide To Trondheim, Norway

Photography by John D. Weigand
Poetry by Penelope Dyan

Whether you live inland on land,
or right next to the sea,
home is where YOU want to be.

You travel by train past a lake of blue.
Thoughts of home seem
to beckon to you.

You chug a chug up and stop
at a train station painted barn red,
You WISH could get off of this train;
however, Trondheim STILL lies ahead!

You see a school with swings.
You miss your VERY best friend.
You ask dad, grumbling,
"When will THIS trip FINALLY end?"

In town, Mom sees a beautiful railing
of black and gold.
"We will be going home soon,
so don't worry," YOU are told.
It is as if YOUR mom is in YOUR head;
and ALL of YOUR thoughts,
SHE has seen AND has read!

The buildings are VERY colorful!
This is quite true.
But it seems like right now,
you are feeling quite blue!

A statue of a deer and its fawn
FINALLY makes you smile!
And you don't even THINK about home
for a long, long while!

And as lovely as it can be,
(like a picture postcard)
homes stand THERE on pillars
right THERE on the SEA!
All YOU can do NOW is stop and stare,
as you breathe in deeply
the salty sea air!
And you wonder (if YOU lived there)
AND if it was YOUR wish,
if YOU could go fishing
(right off of that pier)
and catch a great big FISH!
Then Mom could cook that fish in a pot,
making a delicious meal (to eat)
that YOU would like a lot!

Then back down the streets you walk.
You buy some postcards to send home.
And you talk and talk and talk.

You aren't so homesick
after you find a place to play.
In fact,
(you find) you are NOW having
an oh so VERY good day!

You wonder if the boats you see,
(like in Venice, Italy)
are used just like we use cars.
You ask,
"Do moms and dads take their kids
out on the sea
to look up at the stars?"

Then YOU wish you lived HERE
on a sailboat!
And upon the ocean YOU
would float and float and float!
With sails unfurled and unfetterd,
with Mom and Dad you'd be,
ONE with all of nature,
and ONE with ALL of the sea.
Mom interrupts your silent thoughts
and knowingly says to you,
"Wouldnt it be great fun,
if ALL of your dreams came true?"
Smiling, not longing for home anymore,
YOU wonder what (for YOU)
life AHEAD has in store!

"Make your life
a postcard of your dreams.
Make all your dreams
come true!"

Penelope Dyan

www.ingramcontent.com/pod-product-compliance
Ingram Content Group UK Ltd.
Pitfield, Milton Keynes, MK11 3LW, UK
UKHW060134240426
12048UKWH00002B/35